A Step by Step

Wordpress

Tutorial for Beginners

Wordpress 2.7.1

Mati H Fuller

Bigger Vision Books

A Step by Step

Wordpress

Tutorial for Beginners

Wordpress 2.7.1

FIRST EDITION

ISBN 978-0-578-02270-3

Published by Bigger Vision Books
Cover design by Mati H Fuller

Printed by http://www.lulu.com

Other Books
by Mati H Fuller

Beyond the Veil of Delusions,
2nd Revised Edition
A homeopathic psychology book,
printed by http://www.lulu.com
Published by Bigger Vision Books, 2007
ISBN 978-0-6151-7138-8

Desire is Business.

You Have to Do

Something,

Only Then

Will you be Happy

A Bird on the Wings
Chapter #2
Chapter Title: No Mind, No Truth
Question 1

Bhagwan Shree Rajneesh

Acknowledgments

First I would like to thank my friend and editor Dianne Bairstow for patiently reading and editing yet another one of my books. Her efforts to make the book easy to read and understand is much appreciated. A big thanks to Nigell, Holly and Taru for putting up with me while I was working on this project. And another big thanks to the Universe for for always being an unlimited source of inspiration to me. Life is the greatest gift of all!

Table of Contents

Introduction

This is a "how to" book about creating a blog using the latest edition of Wordpress, currently Wordpress 2.7.1. You have probably heard about blogs (websites with dynamic content), since there are millions of people out there who are already blogging. Traditional websites with static content are "out," blogs have become the technology of the future and lots of people will tell you how easy it is to get started! There are many free blog services to pick from, and all you have to do is sign up, and in 5 minutes or less, you can have your blog up and running!

Tempting as it may be, signing up for a free blog service isn't always your best option. Why? Mainly because you won't own your URL (blog address). On a free hosting service, the URL belongs to the host. And if you ever decide to move your blog to a different host, not only is it difficult to do, but you may lose your readers as well since you'll have to change your URL in the process. Besides, setting up a blog *properly* takes a lot more time than just the 5 minutes it took to open the account with a free host, so it is worth having to do it only once.

I didn't realize exactly how much time and effort it takes to set up a blog until I actually created my own. Even though I had bought and read two of the best books I could find about blogging, "Blogging with Moxie" and "Problogger," before I even attempted to create my own blog, there were still so many technical questions to figure out that at some point I almost gave up.

Both of these books contained tons of tips, hints, great advice, and even some tutorial pages, but not nearly enough, at least not for someone as technically challenged as me. I kept wondering how to do all the little details that experienced people already know so well that they assume that you know it, too. They don't understand that if you know *nothing* about computers, whatsoever, you need everything spelled out in great detail to be able to do it. For example, the books will tell you *where* to go and find a new theme (template) for your blog, but not *how* to actually put the new theme into your Wordpress account after you find one that you like. You can probably figure out on your own that it has to be downloaded to your computer in a zip file format first, but then what do you do with it? Does it have to be unzipped before you upload it somewhere? And where does it go? To Wordpress, or to your host? And how do you change the header and the colors in your new template? How do you make Gravatars work for your blog? What exactly are the steps for creating a subscription for an email list and a newsletter? How do you set up your blog for automatic "pinging," automatic backup or send out automatic thank you notes to the people who leave comments on your blog? If you want a professional looking blog, these are things that you need to have, but how do you go about setting it all up, if you don't know anything about computers or blogs??? Questions like this can make you faint just thinking about it! But never fear, this book will unveil all these basic mysteries of blogging with easy step by step instructions.

One of the problems I ran into, when trying to create my first blog, is that most of the tutorials on the web talk about older versions of Wordpress, which was no good to me, since I am using version 2.7.1. This new version of Wordpress is so different that a lot of the information on the web no longer applies. After reading blog forums and searching Google for "how-to" information, I also discovered that I wasn't the only one who didn't have a clue how to set up a blog. Lots of other people were in the same boat as me! The forums were full of questions similar to mine, and either there were no answers at all, or the answers that were posted were so heady and geeky that no normal computer illiterate person could possibly understand a word of what they were saying. These superior computer geeks are obviously so plugged in to the new technology of today that they can no longer explain anything in simple English. Oh, well, maybe I'm just envious...

What I really needed was a good tutorial that could walk me through all this technical stuff step by step. Unfortunately, I couldn't find any tutorials for the latest version of Wordpress, not even on amazon.com! That is when I decided to make one myself, since it dawned on me that if I had to figure it all out, I might as well write down the answers so the information could be shared with others later. The fact is, technology is here to stay. If you don't want to be left behind in the dust, you have to learn at least some of the most basic information, but with a good tutorial, it really isn't that bad!

Introduction

So, what makes this book different? This isn't just a book about the benefits of blogging and all the fun things you can do with a blog. There are so many books out there that are already talking about this. I assume since you bought this book, you already know that blogs are cool, and you are ready to design your own. If that is where you are at, you don't need any more convincing. What you need is a practical, hands-on tutorial that can help you make heads and tails out of the technical world of blogs, without overloading your mind with too much gibberish, and this book will tell you exactly how to do that.

In "A Step by Step Wordpress Tutorial for Beginners," you will learn only what you need to know – no more, no less. The chapters are arranged sequentially, so all you have to do is go through them one at a time. Once you have completed all the chapters that are relevant to your blog, not only will you end up with a fully functional professional looking blog, but hopefully, you will also have some traffic and subscribers, which you can then turn into a potential business over time if you wish.

This Wordpress tutorial is a basic tutorial written in plain English with as little technical mumbo jumbo as possible. It is written for people who are more interested in the blogging part than in the technical "how-to." Go here, open this window, click here, do this... It can't get much simpler! Let's face it! There is no denying that today's technology is complicated and that it takes a lot of accuracy to make it work properly, but with a good step-by-step tutorial, anyone can do it! Trust me! If you can read a cookbook, you are fully qualified to read this book, too. Just follow the instructions like a recipe, one step at a time, and before you know it, you'll be blogging away! So, if you are ready to start your first blog, don't hesitate! Even if you know nothing about blogs, just jump in, get your feet wet, and I'll teach you how to swim!

Free Blog or Self-hosted?

If you wonder what a "host" is, think of it as a company that provides a space for your blog on the internet. This makes it easy for anyone searching the net to find it. There are two types of hosts; some offer a free blog hosting service and others charge a monthly fee to host your blog. This is what we call "self-hosted blogs."

The first decision you have to make before creating a blog is whether you want a free blog or a self-hosted blog.

The advantages of free blog services are:
1) They are free, obviously.
2) They are easy to set up.
3) Some allow you to change the header.
4) You get to see if you like blogging without having to get financially involved right away.

The disadvantages of free blog services are:
1) Limited amount of themes to choose from.
2) Long URLs (website addresses) that are difficult to remember.

3) Less options for personalizing your theme.
4) You don't own your URL, so if you want to move your blog to a self-hosted service later, you'll loose your URL, as well as your readers.
5) Moving a blog that is full of posts is a complicated undertaking.
6) Remember, that the most efficient way to do things, is doing them only once.

Considering the fact that it doesn't have to cost more than about $5.00 per month to host your blog, it doesn't really make any sense to use a free blog service. It is fine, if you just want your blog to be a way to connect with your family or friends, but if you have other ambitions for the future life of your blog, it is better if you start out on the right foot by choosing a good paid host from the very beginning. Then you won't be sorry later, it is as simple as that.

As soon as you have made your decision about whether or not you want a free blog or a self-hosted blog, the next thing you have to do is find a name for your blog (URL).

Picking a Name for Your Blog

Picking a name for your blog is always eas-ier said than done, since most of the good URLs are already taken. The ideal URL should be short, simple and easy to remember. The search engines love it if you can put a few keywords into the URL, too. The URL should ideally either describe some aspect of your blog, or it should represent you as a person in some way. If you can't think of a name that covers all these aspects, don't worry. There are so many websites out there now that it is almost impossible to find a perfect name, so just do the best you can, and find something that appeals to you.

Finding a good name for your blog always takes time, so don't try to rush into it. It is better to wait until you find a name that feels right to you, than to end up with something you won't be happy with. Put your creative thinking hat on and keep your thoughts coming. Have a pad and paper handy, and write down anything that pops into your head. It is important not to be too critical, or you'll end up talking yourself out of having a blog altogether. Just let your thoughts flow freely, and have a good laugh once in a while when you come up with something really silly. (Don't be embarrassed, nobody else will know!)

Once you have your list going, the next thing you have to do is to find out if any of these fabulous new blog names are actually available. You can go to places like http://www.register.com or http://www.GoDaddy.com and search for available URLs. Just put your new blog name into the search box, click search, and it will instantly tell you if the name is already taken, or if it is available for purchase. I would recommend getting a .com name if you can, since they are more common (although harder to find these days).

Remember not to make your URL too long. Something like http://www.this-is-my-first-blog-and-I-love-it.com is way too long. Try to avoid names that have too many hyphens or underscores as well, since they are hard for people to remember, and they may look like spam to some of the spam filters.

If you get stuck and can't think of anything that isn't already taken, here is a trick that I use sometimes. Go and ask a child if they can think of a cool name for your blog, and you'll be surprised how many wild and wonderful blog names they can think of in almost no time at all. Children are so much more creative than we are, and they can be great resources of inspiration and ideas when your own ideas run out. Even if you don't use any of the blog names they come up with, their creative combinations of words might still inspire you to think up something totally new. So, just keep playing around with ideas until you find a something you like.

Here are a few ideas to keep in mind:

1) You may want to use your own name in your URL, like bobbiesroses.com.
2) If the name you want is taken, you can try to put one underscore or hyphen some-where, like red-rose.com.
3) You can make a noun into a plural, put "the" in front of it, or combine it with some thing unexpected or unusual. Example: If rose.com is taken, try roses.com, or therose garden.com or even something strange and unusual like velvet-rose.com.

Once you find an available URL that you like, it is time to look for a good host. You can often buy the URL directly from your host, and some hosts even offer a free URL, so it is best to find the host first, and then sign up for a hosting plan and URL at the same time.

There are many hosts to choose from, and choosing the right one is not an easy task. After doing a lot of research, I was able to find a host that fit all my criteria, which were: free, unlimited customer service, one click Wordpress installation, one free URL and unlimited additional URLs per account, a low monthly fee, and a high rating on many of the host reviews on the internet. If you want to know which host I picked, please visit my blog for a detailed description of who they are and what they have to offer:
http://www.fabulouslycheeky.com/my-favorite-web-host

This company has the best hosting service I have ever found, and I can highly recommend them! Their customer service deserves at least 10 stars, and I am very happy to let them host all of my URLs.

Picking a Name for Your Blog

If you choose to go with a different host, please make sure that your preferred host also offers one-click Wordpress installation, preferably with a software installation service called "Simple Scripts," and a control panel called a cPanel, since that is what the information in this book is based upon.

What is Your Blog About?

If you want to write a journal type of blog, and you don't care if anyone can find it on the internet, you don't have to read this chapter, but if you want you blog to be easily found, it is important to do a little bit of research. Personally, I prefer to do this even before I buy the URL, because if you realize that your URL needs to be changed, you still have time to do so.

My very first website got straight to the top of the search engines under the category "one of a kind clothing," and boy was I proud! I sat back and waited with excitement for orders to be coming in every day, and wondered how I would be able to keep up with the demand. But nothing happened. Not even a single order. WHY??? The answer was very simple. I was on top of a category that nobody searches for, that's why.

If you don't want the same thing to happen to your blog, you need to know what people are searching for before you create your blog. Ideally, you need to find a niche where there is a lot of demand and very little supply.

It took a long time for me to really understand what a niche was until someone explained it to me like this: A niche is a problem that you can provide a solution for. Anytime you hear people complain about something, you might be looking at a niche market. So if you can find a group of people who want something that you can supply, and you find that many people want it, but few people offer it, you are in luck. Finding a niche like this makes it much easier to succeed.

So, what does this have to do with your blog? Two things; if you can talk about issues that people are interested in, people are more likely to read your blog, and if you are interested in selling products, you first need to know what people want. In both cases, you need to find out what people are searching for on the net, as well as how many other sites that are offering the same service or product that you have in mind. If lots of people want something that is easily available, that's no good because your competition will be too great. The trick is to find something that many people want, but very few have to offer. This is not an easy thing to find, but there is a site that will help you figure all this out called Wordtracker.com.

This site tracks what people search for on the search engines, which can be very useful information for you to know. It has a free service and a paid one, and I have tried both. If you just want to check on a list of keywords to see if anyone searches for them, you only need the free service. But if you want to look for an unexpected niche that you may not even have thought about, the paid service is better. The paid service will help you brainstorm and give you ideas for words and combinations of words that will help your blog be more visible on the net. It can give you ideas about what to write, what categories you need and what products to offer, if any.

The good thing about Wordtracker is that it can save you time and money by taking some of the "trial and error" out of the equation. Here are some advantages of using Wordtracker.com:

1) You can figure out what people want before you set up your blog.
2) Wordtracker can help you discover niche markets.
3) Wordtracker can give you a list of prominent keywords to use on your blog.
4) These keywords can be used to optimize your blog for the search engines by putting them in your titles, categories and throughout the text.
5) Knowing the right keywords to use can help your blog gain more visitors and better search engine positioning.
6) More visits equal more opportunities for expansion on different levels, especially when it comes to making a profit.

If you want to try the free version of Wordtracker, go to http://freekeywords.wordtracker.com/. You can use this service as much as you want without paying a penny, so it is a good idea to add it to your favorites.

I would suggest that you play around with Wordtracker for a while before you sign up with your host. If you find that there is a demand for what you are planning to offer in your blog, you can go to your host and sign up right now. But if there is no demand for what you are offering or planning to write about, you might need to reconsider both the content of your blog and your URL.

You may think that all this planning is a pain and a hassle that you don't want to be bothered with, but if you don't think some of these things through, and do a little research before jumping in with both legs, you might end up with a blog that nobody will find, and then, what is the point of all the efforts you have put in? If you look at it that way, whatever time you put into planning and finding clarity now, will pay off in the long run in more ways than one. So, be patient and prepare yourself to spend some time with Wordtracker today. I promise you, learning what people are actually searching for is often an eye opening experience!

Sign Up With a Host

Are you ready to sign up with a host? Good! This is the easy part. Go to your host of choice, or if you wish, you can check out my favorite host at http://www.fabulouslycheeky.com/my-favorite-web-host

On the home page, look for "Domain Check" first. Put your blog name into the search box and click "Next." If your host offers URL privacy, you can tick it off if you like. Normally, anyone can do a "whois" search on your URL and read all your private information, such as name, address, phone number and email address. If you want to do a whois-search to see for yourself what it is like, go to http://www.whois.net and put your favorite website's URL into "WHOIS Lookup." Click "GO" and see what happens! If this web owner doesn't have privacy set up, you can access all their private information! If you don't want this to happen to you, you should definitely request PRIVACY from your host.

My favorite host offers privacy as a free service, so if anyone searches your URL, they will only find your host name, and if they want to get in touch with you, they have to go through your host. The host won't give them any of your personal information, they will just send you a message and then you decide if you want to contact them back. Personally, I think it is a good idea to keep your address and phone number private, unless you have a store front and you want to attract customers.

If your URL is still available, your host will give you the option to get the name and sign up for their service. Decide how much of a commit-ment you want, 3 months, 6 months, a year or more, and sign up. It usually takes a while to get a blog up and running, so I would suggest that you sign up for at least one year to start. That gives you enough time to figure it all out, and after a year, you can re-evaluate.

Note: It is a good idea NOT to tick the "Automatic Renewal" box during the signup process. If you have it on automatic renewal, you have to send them a cancellation notice in writing at least 10 days before it renews, or they'll charge you for another year (or whatever time you origi-nally signed up for) and there is nothing you can do about it. If you **take it off automatic**, they will send you an email reminder ahead of time before your account expires, and then you have a choice whether or not you want to renew.

After you have signed up with a host, you will receive emails with confirmation and upload information. You may have to click on certain links to confirm your subscription, so make sure you read them and follow their instructions. Whatever you do, DON'T DELETE THEM! You might need this information later!

After you are done with your signup proc-ess, the best thing to do is to make a new email folder with your host name or blog name on it, and move all your blog related emails into this folder. That way, you'll always know where they are in case you should need this information in the future, and you'll have a safe place to put all your future blog related emails as well.

Install Wordpress With Simple Scripts

After you have signed up with your host, it takes a day or two before your URL can be found on the internet. Open your internet browser and put your full URL into the address bar at the top like this: http://www.yourdomain.com. When your URL is up, you will see a generic page saying something about your website being under construction. When this happens, you can go ahead and install your Wordpress blog software.

If you use a host that offers Simple Script one step installation, the whole process is very easy.

1) Log into your host account. This will take you to your host's cPanel.

2) Scroll down to "Software/Services" and find the square Simple Scripts logo.

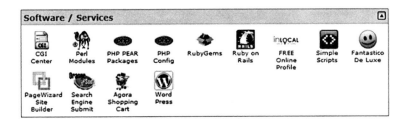

3) Click on Simple Scripts.

4) Then click on the Wordpress logo on the next page, and then "Install Now."

5) On the next page, under "General configuration," choose the latest version of Wordpress. Where it says "Where would you like Wordpress installed," put your URL into the first box and leave the second box empty.

6) Under "Additional Options," give your site a name and then un-tick the box that says "Generate me an Administrator Login."

By un-ticking this box, you get to choose your own login name and password (you can put in whatever you want.)

7) Make sure to tick the box that says "Automatically Create a New Database." This saves you the hassle of having to do it yourself!

8) Then read through the terms conditions and service agreements, tick the little boxes, click "Complete" and you are done!

One-click technology is awesome, isn't it? You don't have to mess around with creating MySql databases or anything like that because Simple Scripts will do it all for you! Simple is the way to go!

Now, you can go on the net and open up your URL, and you'll be able to visit your blog! Don't feel disappointed when you see it. The page that you see is just a Wordpress default page, which is not too exciting, I know. But don't worry, I'll show you how to change that in the next chapter.

Change Your Wordpress Theme

To change the look of your blog, you first need to look for a theme that you like. A theme is simply a blog layout template. With Wordpress 2.7.1 it is very easy to change themes. Here is what you do:

First, open your blog URL and login to your Wordpress account. You'll find a login button somewhere on the blog page itself. After logging in, you'll see a button on your blog that says "Dashboard." Click this button and you are now in your Wordpress dashboard.

Scroll down the dashboard menu until you see "Appearance" and click on "Themes." Here you will see two Wordpress default themes.

In the screen print above, you'll also see my favorite theme "Techozoic Fluid" by Jeremy Clark listed. Why do I love this theme?

Techozoic Fluid is unbelievably user friendly. It comes with an options menu which allows you to choose either a two or three column design. You can easily change the header and the colors of the text, links and sidebars, and you don't even have to see any scary html! Jeremy Clark also offers other themes, so you might want to check them out, too.

Anyway, if you don't jump for joy over the two Wordpress default themes, just scroll down a bit to where it says "Get More Themes" and click on "Wordpress Theme Directory," and you'll find thousands of great themes to choose from (including Jeremy Clark's themes). But, before you go looking for a theme, you first need to decide what exactly you are looking for. Do you want your theme to have 2 or 3 colums? Are you going to want any advertising on your blog in the future? If so, you might want a 3 column theme, so you'll have two sidebars in addition to your blog posts. If you don't care about advertising, a 1 or 2 column theme is probably fine.

And, how technical do you want to get? Do you want to put your own header in? Do you know how to create a jpg for a header in a photo program? If you don't, the easiest thing to do is to find a theme you like and simply use it as it is, without making any changes to it. Wordpress offers lots of really beautiful themes, so it shouldn't be too difficult to find one that you like that doesn't have to be changed.

If, however, you want your blog to have a more personal flavor, a new header is a good idea. You can even hire someone to do it for you, if you wish. If the person you hire also happens to know Wordpress, you are in luck. Perhaps you can bribe him or her into installing the header for you as well! If that doesn't work, you'll have to install it yourself, which means that you'll need to prepare yourself to encounter some html (unless you choose one of Jeremy Clark's more user friendly themes). Anyway, if you are planning on customizing, make sure you search for a customizable theme.

Once you find a theme you like, click on the theme link. On the next page, click on "Preview" if you wish, then "Download" and "Save."

I like to put the saved file on the desktop, so it is easy to find it later. It is downloaded as a "zip-file," but don't worry – you don't have to unzip it yet!

After you download the theme to your desktop, go to your host and log in. In my favorite web host, (http://www.fabulouslycheeky.com/my-favorite-web-host), which is what this book is based upon, I go to my cPanel, then scroll down to "Files" and click on "File Manager."

In the next window, tick off "Web Root (public_html/www)," put the name of your directory (website URL) into the little window and click "GO."

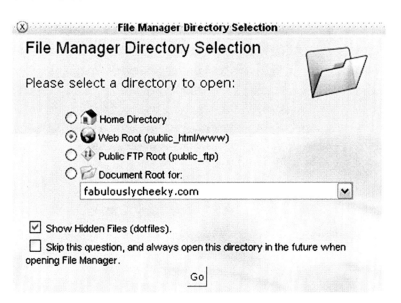

This will open your file manager. Scroll down your left sidebar and click on "public_html." Then click on your blog URL, "wp-content," and then "themes." **This is where you need to upload the theme zip-file on your desktop to.**

Uploading your zip-file is easy. Look at the tool bar on the top of the page in your host and you'll see a symbol that says "Upload." Click it, then click on "Browse," pick the zip-file from your desktop and click "Upload."

After your zip-file shows up in your web files (the logo looks like a small cardboard box), highlight it and click "Extract" from the toolbar above, and it will instantly unzip it (now the cardboard box is open).

After your theme has been unzipped, it will automatically show up in your Wordpress dashboard. Log back into Wordpress and go to

"Appearance," click on "Themes" and you should be able to see your new theme next to the default ones. Pretty nifty!!!

In Wordpress 2.7.1, changing themes is super easy. Just click on the thumbnail of the theme you want. It will show you a preview of what your blog will look like with that theme. If you like it, click on "Activate" in the top right corner of your theme, and that's it! Voila, you blog has a new look! Now we just have to make it yours...

Customize
Your Theme

If you like your theme just the way it is, you can skip this chapter. If you want to customize, read on.

The first thing you are going to want to change is the header. If you were smart enough to pick one of Jeremy Clark's themes, customizing is super easy.

Log into your Wordpress dashboard and scroll down the menu until you see "Appearance." In this section, you will notice a new menu option relating to your theme. If you used the Techozoic theme, it will say "Techozoic Options." When you click on this link, it will take you to an options menu for that theme. Here, you can decide if you want your blog to have 2 or 3 columns, and if you want one sidebar on each side of your blog text, or if you want your blog entries on the left, and two sidebars on the right. You can also change the background and accent color, link color and link hover color (this is a color change that happens when you hold the mouse over a link).

The color has to be written as a hex code, which is represented by a unique combination of 6 numbers and letters. If you don't know the hex code of the colors you want, click on the link that says "Type a hex color code, or choose one HERE," and a small window appears with lots of colors in it. When you hover the mouse over a color in this window, it will show you the color and the hex code at the bottom of the window. This makes it very easy to pick a color you like and fill the corresponding hex color code into the theme options menu.

When it comes to the header, Jeremy Clark gives you many options. You can choose one of the 3 headers that are supplied with the theme, you can rotate the 3 headers randomly, or you can upload your own.

If you choose to use your own header image, you must choose the "Defined Here" option in the drop down menu at the bottom of the page. Then save the changes you have made and go and create your new header. If you need to know the size of the header, click the link that says "see notes," and also make sure you save the header as a jpg file at 72dpi (dots per inch).

I am not going to tell you how to make your own header jpg since there are too many different photo programs out there and I don't know which one you have. Either you know how to do it, or you can hire someone to do it for you. If you need a picture for your header, put "stockphotos" into Google search and you'll have lots of companies to choose from.

TIP: Don't put text on your jpg. The search engines can't read jpg text, so it is basically useless to put any text on your picture.

Once you get your header made and saved as a jpg file at 72dpi, you need to upload it to your

host first. (Make sure you have called it something simple, such as header.jpg). This is what
you do:

Go to your web host and log into your
cPanel and then scroll down to the Files menu.

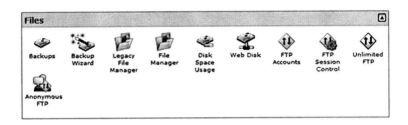

Click on "File Manager," then tick off
"Web Root (public_html/www), fill in your URL in
the box and click "GO."

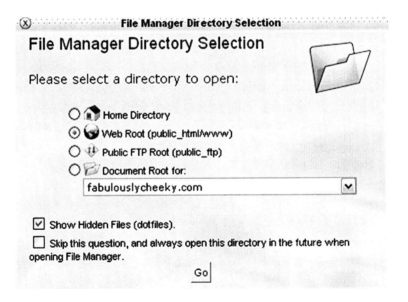

In "File Manager" click on "public_html."
Next click on your URL, then "wp-content,"
"themes," the name of your theme, in my case
"techozoic-fluid," then "images," and "headers."

This is where the header has to be uploaded to. Now look for the "Upload" icon at the top of the page and click it, then "Browse," find your header on your hard drive and click "Upload" again. In just a few seconds, it will show up in your files, as "header.jpg."

Now, log back into your Wordpress dashboard, go to "Appearance" and click on the options menu for your theme again. This time, scroll down to "Header Image URL." Here, you have to put in a path to where your host keeps your header files so Wordpress can find it. If you use my favorite web host (which I hope you do), the path is written like this:

http://www.yourwebsite.com/wp-content/themes/techozoic-fluid/images/headers/header.jpg

NOTE: If you don't use the techozoic-fluid theme, make sure you put the name of your chosen theme into the html instead. For example:

http://www.yourwebsite.com/wp-content/themes/prime-press/images/header.jpg

Then click "Save Changes," and if all goes well, you should be able to see both the new header and the color changes you made when you visit your blog. If you don't like the way it looks, go back, make some more changes and try it again. You may have to upload your header a few times, until you can get the header and the template text to look good together.

If you didn't install one of Jeremy Clark's themes, changing the header is a bit more complicated. **The first thing you have to do is go and look for information about what size the header has to be.** Different themes have this information listed in different places, so **you just have to just look for it somewhere in your theme information.** Once you find it, create your header and upload it to the right place in your host (use the directions described in the text above).

Once you have uploaded your header jpg to the right directory, log into your Wordpress dashboard and go to "Appearance" and click on "Editor." Now you'll see some scary looking text in a window, and a menu on the right with different templates you can edit. Look for a template called "Header" and click on the link. Now the header html will show up inside the window. (Html is the language that computers understand.) If you want your new header to show up on your blog, you need to change some of the html in your header template.

Start reading the gibberish until you see something like **<div id="header_img">** and further down **</div>**. (Don't worry if it doesn't look exactly the same, it is possible that it just says <div id="header">, which is fine.) Highlight everything in between **<div id="header_img">** and **</div>**, and replace it with this code instead:

<img src="<?php bloginfo('template_url'); ?> /images/header.jpg" width="1000" height="200" alt="<?php bloginfo('name'); ?> header image 1" title="<?php bloginfo('name'); ?>" />

Make sure you write it **exactly** like this, since every little dot and space is important and has to be there if you want it to work!

NOTE: In the html above, you will see that width and height is set to 1000 and 200. This is the size of the header image for Techozoic-Fluid. If you need a different size header image, then **you must change these numbers to correspond with your particular header size** before pasting it into the header html. For example, if your header jpg is 770 x 140, you'll have to write 770 instead of 1000, and 140 instead of 200, before pasting the html into your header template. This should make your header appear.

Next you might want to change some of the colors on you blog, and this process is a bit more tricky. If you picked a customizable theme, hopefully they provided you with a Custom.CSS file so you don't have to change anything on the original stylesheet. (A stylesheet, or a CSS-file, contains information about things you find on every page of your blog, such as text or background color, etc.)

Scroll down the template menu and click on your Custom.CSS file, if there is one. (If there isn't, you might consider a different theme just to make it easier for yourself.)

If you want to change the color of the theme's navigation buttons, look for a section in your stylesheet (CSS file) that says **ul#nav.** Nav means navigation button. Then look for anything that says **color: #number.** The number/letter combination after the pound sign is called **a hex number**, which is basically a letter/numeric description of the color. It may look something like this:

ul#nav li.current_page_item a {color:#f7f7f7;

The only thing we have to concern ourselves with here is the number/letter combination after the pound sign, in this case f7f7f7. This is the hex value for a color. If you want to change this to a different color, you have to find the hex value for the new color you want and replace the old value with the new one. You can find hex numbers either in your photo program, or by visiting this site:

http://www.2createawebsite.com/build/hex-colors.html

If you want to change any other colors, just look for **color:#**. The numbers or letters after the #-signs are always hex values. Just make sure you write down what it was before you changed it, in case something doesn't work out, and be careful not to delete anything you shouldn't delete!

By now, you can probably see why I prefer Jeremy Clark's themes to all the other options out there. User-friendliness is his specialty, so for anyone who doesn't quiver with excitement over the possibility of doing surgery on html templates, I highly recommend picking a theme with a more user friendly options menu instead! (Or even better, find a theme you like, and just keep it as it is!)

Plugins and Widgets

Unfortunately, there is a bit of lingo associated with the creation of blogs, and if you want to know what people are talking about, you just have to learn what these words mean.

Wordpress is what they call an "open source" software, which means that it is created by anyone who feels like adding to it. This is why Wordpress keeps changing so often, simply because it is still being created.

Wordpress is a huge computer program that is made to fit many people's different needs, but as we all know, you can never please everyone. Some people have needs that other people don't have, and therefore, someone came up with the idea of making Wordpress customizable by creating plugins, also called add-ons.

A plugin is a very small computer program that can increase the functionality of a much larger program, such as Wordpress. So, if you want Wordpress to do something that the basic program can't do, you simply go and look for a plugin that can do what you want, and then add it to your blog.

Finding a plugin and installing it into your blog is not difficult at all because the newest version of Wordpress is actually very user friendly. This is what you do:

First, log into your Wordpress dashboard. Then scroll down the menu on the left until you see "Plugins." Click on "Add New" and a page with a search box opens up. Here, you can search for whatever plugin you want. If you don't know what to search for, just click on one of the links on the top, like the one that says "Newest" or "Recently Updated" and you'll get almost 200 pages of plugins to choose from.

NOTE: Because you are using the very latest version of Wordpress, you are going to have a bit of a problem finding plugins that are actually compatible with your blog. When you click on the name of the plugin that you want, it may have some kind of warning on it that it hasn't been tested on your version of Wordpress yet. Personally, I got really tired of looking for something that was compatible with the latest version since most of the cool plugins were not, so I started installing them anyway. And, so far, so good, none of the plugins I chose have given me any problems.

Installing a plugin is super easy. When you find one that you want, just click "Install." This takes you into an installation page where you can read more about what the plugin can do before you install it. It is a good idea to read both the description and the installation instructions before downloading it because it will tell you if it is an easy installation, or if you need to mess with html.

If you choose to install the plugin, simply click the "Install Now" link in the upper right corner. This will put your new plugin into your Wordpress menu under "Plugins." Click on "Installed" and you'll see your new plugin there under "Inactive Plugins."

Before the plugin will work, you have to activate it. Tick it off, find "Activate" in the drop down menu above and click "Apply," and your plugin will find its way up to the "Currently Active Plugins" menu instead.

For some plugins, this is all you have to do. For others, you'll also see the name of the plugin in your dashboard menu somewhere, which means that you'll have to click on it and fill in some forms manually. It is no big deal – you just have to remember to check the dashboard menu after activating your plugins to see if anything else needs to be done to them.

If you wonder what kinds of plugins you should have in your blog, here are some of the ones that I installed for my blog. I know that these work for Wordpress 2.7.1, even though some of them still have warnings, so don't worry about the warnings. Here are my main recommendations:

1) "All in one SEO pack" – this plugin will help you optimize your blog, as well as your blog posts, for the search engines. After activating your plugin, you'll also see it in the menu under "Settings," so make sure you click on the link and fill in the information they ask for. In addition, you'll also find a form to fill in at the bottom of the page whenever you write a new post. Here you can fill in title, keywords and description for your post. If you want the search engines to find your site, this plugin is a must.

2) You should probably also have some kind of counter on your blog. I picked a plugin called "Count per Day." This counter shows count per day, yesterday, last weeks, last months etc, and it will also tell you which of your posts people are reading. You'll see a link in the menu under "Dashboard" and also under "Settings." The link under "Settings" has to be filled in with more information, and the "Dashboard" link shows the statistics when you click on it.

3) Another counter that I really like is called "StatPressReloaded." It will show you how many people visited your site, how many feed subscriptions you have (more about feeds in a later chapter), what pages people are visiting, and more. A very useful plugin! This one will show up in your menu at the bottom of each page. To see the stats you just have to click on it. Super easy!

4) Another favorite plugin is called "Thank me Later." This plugin will automatically send people a thank you note for leaving a comment to one of your posts. You can set it to send this message a few hours, days or even weeks after they left the comment, and it will act as a reminder of your blog which can bring one-time readers back.

5) I can also mention a plugin called "Yet Another Related Post." This plugin will provide the readers with related posts, which is a great way to get people to stay in your blog longer and keep reading. This

plugin also shows up in your menu under "Settings," so make sure you click on it and fill in the proper information.

In addition to these 5 basic plugins, I also added some more specialized plugins, which I'll talk more about in the next few chapters.

Adding a Contact Form

It is always good to offer a contact form to your readers so they can contact you privately, if they wish, since some questions aren't suitable for public view. Another good thing about having a contact form is that it also keeps your email address private.

Adding a contact form is a little bit more complicated than adding a normal plugin, simply because your contact form has to be on a static page, which is like a web page, rather than a blog page. So, here is what you do:

First, go to your Wordpress dashboard and find "Plugins" on the menu. Click on "Add New" and search for "contact form." You can pick any one you like, of course, but if you want the one I picked, it is called "Contact Form 7." It is nice and easy to install and use.

Install the plugin and go to your plugins menu to activate it. Normally, this is all it takes to get a plugin to work, but like I mentioned at the top of the page, a contact form has to be on a page of its own.

After your contact form plugin has been activated, scroll down your dashboard menu and find "Pages," and click on "Add New." Write a title at the top, something like "contact" or "contact form," and add this piece of html in the window below:

[contact-form 1 "Contact form 1"]

Then click publish, and you are done.

With Jeremy Clark's themes, the link to this page shows up automatically at the top of the page next to the "Home" and "About" button. If you don't see a link to your new page anywhere on your blog, you are going to have to add a link to this page, or nobody will be able to find it. (Make sure there really is no link before you go to all the effort of adding one!)

To add a link to your new page, you first have to find out what the URL (web address) of this page is. Go to "Pages" in your menu and click on "Edit." Hover your mouse over your "Contact" page title and click on "Edit" (right under the title). At the top of the next page, right under the title, you'll find:

"Permalink: <u>http://www.mywebsite.com/contact</u>

This is the URL that you have to link to if you want people to be able to find your new page (more about permalinks in a later chapter). Copy this URL.

Now, you have two options – you can either add a link to your new page in your header somewhere, or you can add the link to one of your sidebars. Go to "Appearance" and click "Editor." This takes you to where your html pages are. Here, you have to pick either the header.php or one of the sidebars.

If you choose the header, look for other links, such as "Home" and "About," and add the link to your contact page after "About." (If you can't find any links, you can always add it somewhere, just to see what happens. Just make sure you remember what you just did, so you can undo it if it doesn't work.)

I think it is easier to add the link to your sidebar, than to the header, but that is just my own personal preference. Here is the html you need to add somewhere to your php sheet to create a link to your new page:

<li><a href="http://www.mywebsite.com/contact"> <strong>Contact Form</strong></a></li>

(Make sure you replace "mywebsite.com" with the URL that you copied previously). **<li>** is the opening symbol for link, and **</li>** is the closing symbol. Because links often appear in lists, make sure you add your new link after the </li> of the previous link in your php sheet. If you don't want "Contact Form" to appear in bold in your sidebar, just remove **** and ****.

The reason why I wanted to explain in detail how to add an order form is because you have to use the same method if you want to make any kind of static pages in your blog.

Wordpress will allow you to create both parent pages and child pages, which means that you can create a website within your blog that has main pages with sub-pages under it. For example, if your main page is "Flowers," your sub-pages can be different types of flowers.

This way, you can actually create a combination of blog pages with dynamic content as well as static traditional type web pages under the same URL – no problem! There is no need to use some kind of complicated content management system, just stick with Wordpress; it can do it all, you just have to learn how.

Automatic Backup

Here is another great plugin you need to have. Imagine what a bummer it would be, if your blog, with all your great posts, just disappeared some day due to server failure, or whatever! If you don't want the hassle of downloading your whole blog in a zip file to your hard drive every day, all you need is a plugin that can back it up for you automatically!

I found this absolutely awesome plugin called "Wordpress Online Automated Backup." Go to "Plugins," click "Add New" and search for "backup," and you'll find it.

After installing and activating the plugin, it will show up in your dashboard menu at the bottom of your page. Find the symbol for "wpBackup" and click on "Options." On this page, you will be able to create a new site key, which will be needed later in the installation process. This key is also called your **Wordpress key**. Just erase all the numbers you see in the window, and put something that is easier to remember instead. It doesn't have to be numbers; you can write whatever you want. Then save the new key you have just made.

Further down on the same page, under "Restoring Data," it is recommended that you write NO. This is because it is easy to click the restore button by accident, so it is better to leave it off for now. You can always change it to YES at a later time if you should ever need to restore your site, but if you don't need it right now, just write NO, and then save you selection.

Keep scrolling down the page. You want NO memory limit and NO time limit. At the bottom of the page, write your blog URL ending with a forward slash, like this:

http://www.mywebsite.com/

That last little forward slash is very important, so don't forget! But you are not even half done with your installation, yet, so keep on reading!

Now you must open an account with a company called http://www.wordpressbackup.com. Go to the home page and click on "Backup" at the top of the page. After creating your account, you will receive an email with an **activation key**. Copy this **activation key** (or activation code – they are both the same thing). Then, go back to http://www.wordpressbackup.com/backup and click "Activate Account." Enter your user name and **activation key from your email**, and you'll be logged in.

Click the "Sites" submenu and then click "+Add a site." Enter a name for your site. Then enter your URL (web address) and make sure you add a forward slash to the end again, like this:

http://www.mywebsite.com/

Next you have to enter your "**Wordpress key**" – do you remember? The one that you created in your Wordpress plugins page? Yes, that's the one! (Not the activation key that you got in your email!) Paste it in, click "Add it." and then click "Test" to see if the connection is working. If you pass the test, you are done, and your site will be put in line for automatic backup. If you don't pass, you did something wrong and you may have to go over all the steps again!

NOTE: You could have mixed up the two keys – I did that on my first try, so make sure you use the activation key from your email first, and then the Wordpress key next. Just be patient – it's a one time thing! Once it is set up, you can blog away and never have to think about backups again!

If you wonder how you can tell if your site is being backed up regularly, all you have to do is go to your Wordpress dashboard, scroll down to the bottom, find wpBackup and you'll see a little tag next to the symbol. If the tag is green, your site is being backed up regularly. (It will take a day or so before the tag turns from yellow to green, so don't worry, just give it some time.)

If you want to see when it was backed up last, click on wpBackup and it will show you when your last backups were done. Now you can relax and forget all about backups because from here on, it will all happen automatically! Well done!

RSS and Feedburner

Blogging is really "in" these days. There are blogs about pretty much everything under the sun, so whatever your interest is; it is almost guaranteed that you can find a blog about it somewhere. If you have a wide enough range of interests, you may keep an eye on as many as 20 or more blogs, simply because you don't want to miss any interesting posts.

It is easy to imagine how much time it would take to keep track of so many different blogs. Not only would you have to remember each site's URL, but it would also take a lot of time every day to visit so many sites just to see if there were any new posts. This is probably fine if your memory is great and you are just looking for a way to kill time, but most people don't have that much time on their hands. They may have jobs, families, even real friends (not just virtual ones). Because all these eager bloggers were running out of time, some great genius came up with the idea of RSS, which is an abbreviation for "Really Simple Syndication." I like the "Really Simple" part, but what is "Syndication"?

Syndicate means "to organize or administer." RSS is a really simple way to organize or administer your blog content so that it can be distributed to people who want to read it.

Let's go back to the example above and imagine that YOU are the one who is spending all your spare time trying to keep up with the content of 20 different blogs. Wouldn't it be much easier if you could create your own virtual newspaper with headlines from all these different blog posts? Wouldn't it save your day if you could visit just one site and find all the exciting news articles right there? You wouldn't have to remember any other URLs, you wouldn't have to keep visiting all your favorite blogs to see if there were any new posts written, you could just visit your virtual newspaper instead, scan the headlines, and read whatever posts that looked interesting that day. That way, you would be able to keep up on all the good stuff with very little time and effort!

This is exactly what RSS is about. Your blog content is called a feed, and with RSS you can distribute that feed to something called a feed reader (your virtual newspaper) so people can keep up with your posts without having to waste any time checking your site. All they have to do is subscribe to your feed, and then they can just check their feed reader whenever they are in the mood for reading blog posts.

Subscribing to a feed is easy. Just click on the universal feed icon, which looks like this:

Every blog, that offers RSS subscriptions, will have one of these symbols on their blog some-where, and all you have to do is click on it (or if it says RSS, just click on that instead). However, you won't be able to read any feeds unless you sign up with a feed reader first. The easiest way to do this is to sign up for an account with Google, since Google offers a free feed reader. To sign up for a Google account, go to:

https://www.google.com/accounts/NewAccount

This form is so simple that it doesn't need any kind of explanation on my part. Just fill in the information and create your account.

Now that you have your own Google account, you can easily subscribe to anyone's feeds. To see how it works, go to one of your favorite blogs, look for the universal feed icon, click on it and you'll be asked what reader you want to use.

If you have opened a Google account, click on the Google icon. On the next page, click "Add to Google Reader" and you're done. Now, all you have to do, when you want to read feeds from your favorite blogs, is to login to your Google account at

https://www.google.com/accounts/

(If you can't remember this URL, just search for Google Accounts and the page will come up in the search listing).

Now, imagine if your blog became so unbelievably popular that thousands of people subscribed to your feeds. Their feed readers would have to keep checking your blog almost continuously for updated blog entries, and it would totally overload your server. Your blog would be as slow as ebay on the weekends, and your readers would quickly lose interest and go to a faster blog instead. Feed popularity is great, but what can be done about this problem? Simple – use a company called Feedburner to distribute your feeds! This will free up your server and give your RSS subscribers their new feeds almost instantly!

There are many advantages to signing up with Feedburner: The sign up process is simple, they offer easily recognizable RSS icons that you can put on your blog, and they even offer the option of subscribing via email for people who don't feel comfortable with RSS. In addition, Feedburner also tracks and counts how many subscribers you have, and any time you want to see the statistics, you can just log in and click on the "Analyze" tab at the top of the page to check your numbers.

When you signed up for your Google account, you may have also noticed that Feedburner is one of the free services they offer in addition to your feed reader. So, to sign up with Feedburner, just log in to your Google account and click on the

Feedburner icon. Now a page will open where it says "Burn a Feed Right This Instant." Type your blog address (URL) into the window and click "Next." After your address has been validated, Feedburner will give you a code, something like:

http://feeds2.feedburner.com/BlogName

Copy this code and then log into your Wordpress dashboard. Next, you need to install a Feedburner plugin. I used one called "FD Feedburner Plugin" which works fine for version 2.7.1 of Wordpress. Scroll down the dashboard menu to "Plugins" and click "Add New." Search for "Feedburner" and install and activate the one you want.

If you picked the FD Feedburner plugin, you'll see in the dashboard menu under plugins a link to "Feedburner Configuration." Click on this link. On the new page where it says "Redirect my feeds here," and "Redirect my comments feeds here," paste the code that you got from Feedburner into both the boxes.

If your blog is going to have categories, you'll also want to tick off the box that says "Append category slug." This keeps your RSS feeds in categories when it is distributed. Then click "Save" and you're done with the first part of the process. Now you can check your blog to see if your theme offers RSS. Do you see the universal feed icon anywhere?

If you don't see it, and RSS is not available in your widgets either, you need to add an RSS icon to one of your sidebars. (Widgets are also called gadgets or dodaads. They are all the little "things with no names" that appear in your sidebars, like forms, links, blogroll, recent posts, statistics etc. You'll find Widgets in your dashboard menu under "Appearance.")

To add an RSS icon to your sidebar, go back into your Feedburner account and click on the "Publicize" tab at the top of the page. On the next page, scroll down the menu on the left and click on "Chicklet Chooser." This opens a page with lots of different icons. Tick off the one you want and scroll down to the bottom of the page to copy the code that you need for that icon. This code then has to be pasted into one of your side bars in your blog.

To paste your code, log into your Wordpress dashboard, go to "Appearance" and click "Editor." Pick the left or the right sidebar.php file and paste your RSS code somewhere near the top. Scroll down the html and look for <li> and </li>. These are link symbols. Paste your code either before or after one of these link symbols (but not in between!) and see if it shows up in your sidebar where you want it. It may take a bit of trial and error to get it right.

Next, you might want to offer your subscribers the option to subscribe via email in addition to RSS. To activate a Feedburner email subscription, you need to log back into your Google account and click on your Feedburner link. Click on "Publicize" again, and this time, click on "Email Subscriptions" in the menu on the left. Follow the simple steps, and paste your code into one of your Wordpress sidebar templates. You can choose if you want a subscription form, or if you just want subscription via a link.

The advantage of using Feedburner's email subscription is that it is super easy to set it up, it offers double opt-in subscription, and it will automatically send out an email to your subscribers whenever you create a new post. Double opt-in is where people subscribe, and then receive an email where they have to confirm their subscription again. The advantage of double opt-in subscription is that nobody can accuse you of spam when you email them.

After you sign up for email subscriptions with Feedburner, you also need to fill in some information from the sidebar menu in Feedburner. The information under "Subscription Management" and "Communication Preferences" is self explanatory. The next link, "Email Branding" needs a little bit of explanation. On this page, there is a place where you can put in a logo URL so that the emails that are sent out have a logo that relates to your website. This is a good idea, since it will help people recognize that your emails are from your blog.

If you would like your emails to have a logo, this is what you have to do: First, make a logo in a photo program, or get someone to make it for you. The easiest way to create a logo is to just use a piece of your header to make it look similar to your blog header. Make the logo size 200x200 pixels and save it as a jpg. It is ok to save it at 72 dpi.

Next, log in to your host. Scroll down the cPanel to "Files" and click on "File Manager." Then click on "Go," "Public_html" and then "Images." This is where you need to upload your logo to. Now, look in the top bar and find a symbol for "Upload." Click on this symbol, browse for the logo, and it will automatically upload. You should be able to see it in between the other files on that page if the upload was successful.

Once the logo has been uploaded, you need to find your logo's URL so you can add it to your "Email Branding" page in Feedburner. To find the image URL, you need to go back to your cPanel. This time, you need to click on "Legacy File Manager." When the new window opens, click "Go." In the next window, click on the blue folder next to "Images." Now, you should be able to see your logo jpg link. Click on the logo link, and you'll see a menu in the upper right corner. At the bottom of this menu, you will see a URL. This is the logo's URL. All you have to do is click on it, and copy the address in the address bar on the top of the page.

Next, you need to go back to your "Email Branding" page in Feedburner and paste in your logo URL. Then scroll down to the bottom of the page and click "Save." You should now be able to see your logo in your email preview. Your email subscription option is now ready to use. You can test it by subscribing to your own email, and see what happens. You should be getting an email update from your blog, and if you try to write a comment, you should get an email thanking you for the comment as well.

Once you start writing blog entries, Feedburner will automatically check your site on a regular basis. Your new feeds will show up in your subscriber's feed readers within an hour or less, and if people have subscribed via email, they will receive an email notification the same day. If you want Feedburner to distribute your feeds quicker than that, you can set up your Wordpress blog for automatic pinging if you wish (more about pinging in the next chapter).

Pinging and Trackbacks

As you travel through the blogosphere, you may stumble upon blog entries that are so interesting that you almost can't contain yourself – you simply HAVE to write something about what you just read. But, since it wasn't your original idea, you want to give the other author some kind of credit for what you just wrote in your own blog since that is where your inspiration came from. There are two ways of doing that, through pingbacks and trackbacks. The two methods have so many things in common that a lot of people don't even know what the differences are, but I'll try to explain it in simple terms.

Basically, pingbacks and trackbacks are both ways of notifying a web author that someone is linking, or referring, to one of their posts. For example, if Sally reads an inspiring post in Anne's blog, she may be so excited about what she just read that she wants to write an entry about the same issue in her own blog. She puts a link to Anne's post in her entry, since that is where the inspiration came from, and when she clicks "Publish," Wordpress automatically notifies Anne that someone has linked to her post. This is called a pingback. Then Anne's blog software goes back to

Sally's post to check if there really IS a link in her post. If it finds that the link is actually there, the pingback is recorded.

Now, when someone reads Sally's post, they can click on the link to Anne's post if they want to read her entry, too, and likewise, if Anne's readers want to see Sally's post, they can easily enter her blog through the pingback link under Anne's post. This way, the pingback link can increase traffic to both the blogs.

A trackback is another way to notify a website when you publish a post that references someone else's post. While a pingback just shows up as a link on someone's site, a trackback has a link as well as a short excerpt from your entry that will appear on the other website. For example, if Sally wanted to leave a trackback instead of a pingback, she would write a short excerpt of her post in the window below her post entry where it says "Excerpt." Below "Excerpt" there is another window that says "Send Trackbacks To." There, she would write the other blog post's trackback URL.

As soon as she clicked "Publish," Anne's blog would be notified that someone sent her a trackback, and the trackback would show up in her blog with a link and an excerpt from Sally's post. Anne can then decide if she wants to approve or edit the excerpt, and if she approves, it will show up somewhere on her blog so others can click on the link if they wish.

Some people prefer pingbacks over trackbacks because they think pingbacks are more authentic since they have to be double checked before they are approved. Others prefer trackbacks, even though they are more prone to spam, because the excerpt from the post makes the link more interesting so people are more likely to click on it.

Just like pingbacks, trackbacks are also a way of showing the other person how much you appreciated their blog post, and in return, your blog gets a link from their site which can give you better search engine positioning.

So, here is what you have to do if you want to send a pingback or a trackback to someone's post: First, look for a trackback URL so the pingback or trackback will go to the right post. Some sites will have a trackback link (word or icon) under the blog post that you want to link to. If you can't find any icons or links, you might try to click on the post's title instead and see what happens.

If it is a Wordpress blog, and it has pingbacks and trackbacks enabled, clicking on the post title brings up the post in a new page, and the trackback URL is simply the URL you see in the address bar at the top of this page. Copy this URL, and after completing your post and excerpt, scroll down and add the URL in the box under "Send Trackbacks To," then click "Publish," and the other blog is instantly notified.

NOTE: If you have a link in your post, don't put the same link in your trackback box, too, or you'll end up sending a pingback AND a trackback, which can be annoying for the other blog owner. So make sure you send a pingback OR a trackback, and not both!

So, how do you enable trackbacks and pingbacks on your own blog? In your Wordpress menu go to "Posts" and click "Add New." Scroll down to where it says "Discussion," and you'll see a box that says "Allow Comments on This Post," and another box that says "Allow Trackbacks and Pingbacks on This Post." Make sure these are both ticked off.

In addition, you also have to scroll down the dashboard menu to "Settings" and click on "Discussions." Under "Default Article Settings," tick off all three boxes. Under "Other Comment Settings," you can choose if you want your readers to log in to be able to leave comments. This is a matter of personal preference, but I know from my own experience, that if I have to log in to leave a comment, I'd rather not leave a comment at all. It is just too much of a hassle to have to sign in first. But that decision is entirely up to you.

While you are in this page, you might as well go through some of the other settings, too. Then scroll down to the bottom, click "Save," and your blog is ready to receive pingbacks and trackbacks from all your secret admirers!

Technorati

In the early days, when there were no blogs on the internet, the trick was to find a category that people were searching for and then try to optimize your website enough to get it to the top of the search engines for that category. At first, it wasn't too hard; you just had to put lots of keywords in your html and throughout the text. But as more and more websites appeared on the net, getting your site to the top became harder and harder.

The fate of my last website, http://www.homeopathyonline.biz is a good example. Last summer, I decided to put in a huge effort to get the site up to the top of the "homeopathy" category. After a month of tweeking the site any way I knew how, I managed to get it to number 68 on yahoo out of 30 million sites. But, although number 68 is quite an achievement out of 30 million, it wasn't nearly good enough. Unless I could get it to the first or second page, it was basically no good. Most people don't even know what homeopathy is, but even if they do know, do you think they would be willing to search through 7 pages to find a good homeopath? I don't think so! I know I wouldn't!

This is another reason why having a website is pretty much useless these days because if nobody can find your site, you are basically just spinning your wheels and wasting money. Luckily, someone found a great solution to this problem, too. They came up with a totally new type of search engine, one that is aimed towards indexing blog posts, instead of the whole blog. The name of the main one is Technorati.

Technorati indexes your feeds (blog posts), which is a brilliant idea, because what that means is that every post you write has a chance of being found by potential readers. The blog posts can now be indexed separately and be found in lots of mini categories. That way, readers can find your blog almost as soon as you write your first post, even though there are millions of blogs out there. What you have to do is put key words in your blog categories, post titles and blog text.

It is also a good idea to add "tags" before you publish your posts. Tags are keywords that you want the search engine spiders to index your post for, so it is important to feed the spiders some good keywords before you publish any of your posts. There is a place to put your tags in the right sidebar of your post writing page. Just fill in your keyword tags, separated by commas, in the little box and click "Add."

In addition, Technorati also keeps track of how many pingbacks and trackbacks you receive from other blogs. This is called "Authority" in Technorati, and it shows up as a number next to your blog on your Technorati profile page. If you become unbelievably popular at some point, you could even make it to Technorati's top 100 list. If that ever happens, you'll get more traffic than you could ever imagine.

So basically, if you have a blog that you want anyone else to be able to find, **signing up with Technorati is a must!** But, before you sign up, you first need to know if your blog has valid feeds, since Technorati can't index invalid feeds. To see how your blog measures up, go to http://www.feedvalidator.org and put your URL into the box and click "Validate." If you pass the test, it will say "Congratulations, This is a Valid RSS Feed." (If it doesn't pass the test, Feedvalidator will tell you what is wrong and how to fix it).

Once you get the approval from feedvalidator, you can go to http://www.technorati.com and click "Join" in the top right corner. Fill in all the information and create your account. After your account has been created, log in and click on the blog tab at the top of the page. Pick "My Blogs" and then click on "Claim a New Blog" at the bottom of the page. Fill in your URL and click "Begin Claim."

After clicking "Begin Claim," Technorati will create a code for you to put somewhere on your blog. You can put it in a blogpost, or even in your blogroll if you wish. The code has a link to your Technorati profile, so I put mine in my blogroll in the right sidebar of my blog and just kept it there.

To put the link in your blogroll, go to "Links" and click "Add New" in your dashboard menu. Write the name of the link in the first box (Tecnorati Profile), then the URL in the next box, and then a description of the link if you wish (such as Visit my Profile in Technorati). Tick off "Blogroll" and then "Add Link." Now, go back to Technorati and follow their instructions to complete the claim.

Technorati

Claiming your blog confirms that you are the author of the site, and it also gives the web spiders permission to index your feeds for relevant information. And, while you are logged in to Technorati, you might as well upload a picture of yourself, too, and write a very short description about yourself and your blog. This is for your profile so people can get their curiosity quenched about who you are and what your blog is about. If you wish, you can even send Technorati a manual "Ping" just for fun of it, by clicking the "Ping" button under "Claimed Blogs."

OK, so you signed up with Technorati and you claimed your blog, but you are still not totally done. Just one more thing: If you don't want to go to your Technorati account and ping them manually every time you write a post, you can set up your Wordpress blog to ping them automatically, instead. In addition, there are many other companies similar to Technorati that you should also ping. Here is a list of the main ones:

> http://rpc.pingomatic.com/
> http://rpc.technorati.com/rpc/ping
> http://blogsearch.google.com/ping/RPC2
> http://ping.weblogalot.com/rpc.php
> http://search.yahooapis.com/SiteExplorerSe
> rvice/V1/ping?sitemap=http://www.yahoo.com
> http://rpc.weblogs.com/RPC2
> http://ping.feedburner.com

As you can see, Technorati is there, as well as Feedburner, Google, Yahoo and a few others. Copy all of these URLs and login to your Wordpress dashboard. Scroll down to "Settings" and click on "Writing." Go to the bottom of the page and paste all these URLs into the window under "Update Services."

NOTE: Each URL has to be on a separate line, or it won't work right!

Then click "Save Changes" and you are done! Now, take a deep breath, turn off your computer and go for a walk! You definitely deserve a break!

Gravatars
and Wavatars

One of the coolest things about blogs is the fact that they are open for people to leave comments to your posts. It is fun when someone responds and you can create some kind of discussion, but it is too bad that you don't have a clue who you are talking to. You may not want to put a picture of your real face next to every post you write, but what if you could have some kind of picture or symbol to represent you – at least then, people could recognize you by your image, and you could still keep your privacy intact.

Some blogs let you upload an avatar image when you join their forums. But if you are participating in many blogs or forums, it can easily become a bit of a hassle to have to log in and upload avatars everywhere you go.

Again, someone thought of a really great solution. What if you could have an avatar image that was associated with your email address? This is what a gravatar is. Gravatar stands for "Globally Recognized Avatar." Basically, if your gravatar is associated with your email address, it will show up anytime you leave a comment on someone's blog, provided their blog supports gravatars.

Getting a gravatar is easy and fun, and if you allow gravatars on your blog, then anyone, who leaves a comment, will have a unique picture next to their entry, too. So, if you want to get a gravatar, the first thing you have to do, is go to your host and create an email address for your blog. It can be something simple, like username@yourwebsite.com. If you already have an email address that you check every day, you can simply forward the mail from your new email address to your old one, so you don't have to visit both to get your mail. This is what you do:

First, log in to your host account. Scroll down the cPanel dashboard until you see "Mail" and click on "Email Accounts." Put in a name for your new email account, put in your passwords and click "Create." Then go back to your cPanel under "Mail" and click on "Forwarders," then "Add Forwarder." A form opens up, where you need to fill in the email address you want to forward, and the email address you want to forward your mail to. The email address you want to forward TO can be outside your host, so it is ok to forward it to a hotmail account, a yahoo account, or whatever you choose. Then click "Add Forwarder" at the bottom of the page, and you're all set.

Now, you have to get yourself a picture. You can either use a picture of yourself, or you can go on the net and look for a small picture or symbol that you like. Once you find something that appeals to you, download it to your hard drive.

When you are ready to create your gravatar, go to http://www.gravatar.com and sign up for an account. It is the easiest thing; all they need is your email address, and then click "Signup." Log in to your account, click "Add a New Image," and upload the image you saved on your hard drive.

Next, you have to install a plugin called "Wordpress Gravatar" (also called WP-Gravatar). Log into your Wordpress dashboard and go to "Plugins" and click "Add New." Search for "gravatar" and you'll get lots of options. Install and activate the WP-Gravatar. And while you are here, go ahead and install a plugin called "Wavatars" as well. The gravatar plugin will make it possible for people's gravatars to show up on your site, and the wavatar plugin will create avatars for people who don't have gravatars. That way, anyone who leaves a comment on your blog will have some kind of picture associated with their email address. The gravatar and the wavatar plugin complement each other, and they both work with the latest edition of Wordpress.

Now scroll down your dashboard menu to "Settings" and click "Discussions." Scroll down to "Avatars" and tick off "Show Avatars." Under "Maximum Rating," tick off the maximum rating you are willing to allow in your blog (such as G, or PG), and under "Default Avatar" tick off "Wavatar," then "Save Changes."

NOTE: Nobody is going to tell you this, but you won't get gravatars to work properly in your blog unless you also go in and adjust some of the information in your Wordpress profile. Log in to your Wordpress menu, go to "Users" and click on "Your Profile." Here, you'll find a section where it says "Contact Info." Make sure you fill in the new email address you just created, as well as your domain name. Once these are linked, gravatars will work. And, while you are in this page, you might as well fill in your biographical information, too, and then click "Update Profile."

Before you can test your gravatar, there is one more place you need to fill in. In your Wordpress menu, go to "Settings" and click on "Wavatars" and you'll see a page that has wavatar options. Under "Configuration," tick off "Automatic Placement," under "Size," write 80, then tick off "Gravatar Support," and next, put in the rating levels (G or PG etc) and decide what should happen if the user doesn't disclose his email address. Click "Update Options" and you're all done!

Now, you can go back to http://www.gravatar.com and test your gravatar. Log in, and click on the "Check This Gravatar" link. If you pass the test, you should be able to see your gravatar next to every post you write. If you don't, go over all the steps again, and make sure you didn't forget to do any of them.

Wordpress Settings

You may be wondering by know when you can start writing some blog posts. You are almost ready, I promise, but first we have to go through the Wordpress menu and get all the necessary fields filled in.

The first thing on the menu is "Post." Click on "Edit" and you'll see a sample post that can be deleted. Hover the mouse over the title, and you'll see a delete button.

Next go to "Add New." Scroll down this page to "Discussion," and make sure you tick off "Allow comments on this post," and "Allow track-backs and pingbacks on this post" if you haven't already done that.

Next click "Tags" on the dashboard menu. Here you can add keywords for your blog, if you wish (or you can do it whenever you write a post). But first, you might want to check with http://freekeywords.wordtracker.com/ and see what people are searching for so you can create more useful tags. Put your keyword under "Tag Name," and under "Tag Slug" you write the same thing, but with small letters and hyphens. Make sure you put hyphens between the words in the slug if there is more than one word. For example, if the tag name is "Paper Clips," the slug would be "paper-clips." Then click "Add Tag."

Last, click "Categories." Here you can add categories to your blog. Categories are important, so again, make sure you put proper keywords in them. Under "Category Name," put the name that you want. Under "Category Slug," try to put something slightly different, because if you don't, it can create some pretty weird URLs if you decide to add child category pages later (a child category is basically a sub category.) For example, if your category name is "Fashion," the slug can be "cool-fashions" just to keep it a tiny bit different.

Under "Category Parent" put "none" if this is a main category page. If it is a sub category, or child page, you have to pick a parent page from the drop down menu. Write a description if you wish, and then click "Add Category."

Go to the next step on your dashboard menu, which is "Media." Skip this for now. The "Library" part usually holds pictures, and right now, there are no pictures.

Next, go to "Links" on your menu and click "Edit." Here, you will find lots of sample links that come with your theme. You can delete these if you wish. If you want to add a new link to your blog-roll, click "Add New" and fill in name, web address and description and click "Add link." You'll also see a link for "Link Categories." This will only show up if your theme supports link categories. The Jeremy Clark themes don't at this point, so all your links will automatically end up in your blogroll.

Keep scrolling down the menu to "Pages" and click "Edit." Here, you will find a sample "About" post and you'll also see the contact page you made previously. Open the "About" post, delete the sample text and write your own. If you want to upload a picture of yourself, it is pretty easy. Where it says "Upload/Insert" above the post writing window, you'll see an icon that looks like a picture. Click on it, and it will let you upload a picture from your hard drive. It will make it whatever size you want, and you can also decide how you want to position the picture in your entry. Then click "Update Page."

The next thing on the menu is "Comments." This is where you have to go to moderate comments. Right now, you can skip this, since you don't have any comments yet.

Keep scrolling, and you'll come to "Appearance." Here, you need to click on "Widgets." Click on "Show all Widgets" at the top, and then go through them. If you want any of them in one of your sidebars, pick the sidebar you want from the drop-down menu and just click "Add" and then "Save Changes." You definitely want RSS, archives, categories and blogroll, and perhaps also recent comments, yet another related post (YARPP), statpress, and statpress top posts. There are other options, too, such as tag cloud and calendar. Play around until you figure out what you want, save your changes, skip "Plugins" and go to "Users."

Under "Users," click "Your Profile" if you haven't already filled out this page. This was the page that you had to go through when you were setting up your blog for gravatars.

The next thing on the menu is "Tools." Whenever you want to look for upgrades to Wordpress, you can click on "Upgrade." You'll also see a link to your contact form page. Click this and make sure you put your new email address under "Mail to." Then click "Save."

The last thing on your menu is "Settings." Click on "General," and fill in your blog title, tagline, URL and email. The tagline can either be a funny subtitle, or it can be a few keywords describing what your blog is about. Leave the calendar and time settings as they are and click "Save Changes."

Then go to "Writing." Under "Writing Settings," make sure you set the "Default Post Category" and "Default Link Category." If you don't have any preferences, just leave the default post category as "Uncategorized" and the default link category as "Blogroll." Under "Remote publishing" tick off both boxes. Leave the rest of the page alone, and save your changes.

Next, click on "Reading." Here you can choose if you want your front page to display your latest posts or a static page. Set the blog pages and syndication feeds to show 9 posts instead of the default, which is 10 posts. This is recommended because the default of 10 can sometimes create problem with your theme, perhaps due to some kind of bug. "For each article in a feed," tick off "Full text." Then save changes.

The next link is "Discussions." This page was hopefully filled out when you previously allowed pingbacks and trackbacks and when you filled in the avatar settings. (If you didn't do it previously, now is a good time.)

Leave the "Media" settings alone and go to "Privacy Settings." Here you tick off the level of privacy you want for your blog.

Next, go to "Permalinks." A permalink is a permanent URL for the pages that hold your blog posts. The default setting in Wordpress is not very user friendly, so I chose to tick off "Numeric." Then save changes.

Leave "Miscellaneous" alone, and make sure you fill in all the information that is needed for all your plugins, if you haven't already done so.

Now, you are all done and ready to start writing posts if you wish! If you are not sure how, you might want to check the next chapter first.

How to Write a Post

This is the easy part. Just log into your Wordpress dashboard, go to "Posts" and click "Add New." Write the title to your post in the first box at the top of the page. In the next box, you write your post entry. If you want to go fancy and add a picture, you'll see a picture icon above your post writing window that will allow you to upload a picture. You can also make your post content easier to read if you add bold or italics in places. All you have to do is highlight whatever you want in bold, and then click the "b" in the menu above. If you wish italics, click the "*i*" instead.

In the top menu, you'll also see a blue symbol that says "link." Clicking on this symbol allows you to link your posts together so that people can easily go from one post to the next. At the bottom of each post, you can write something like "Next Post" or "Previous Post" and link it to the appropriate post. This is how you link posts together by using permalinks:

A permalink is a permanent link to a page that holds one of your posts; so basically, every post has their own URL on a static page. In the last chapter, you went in to "Settings/Permalinks" and set the permalinks to "Numeric" to give it a more user friendly structure. Now, imagine you have written your first two posts, and you want to link them together – how do you do this?

First you have to find the permalink for each post. Go to "Post" and click "Edit" and you'll see both your posts listed. Now, click on the title of the first one, and you'll see a long URL with a three digit number at the end. Write down this number. Do the same for the other post, and write down that number, too.

Now, go back into your first post and highlight where you wrote "Next Post" at the bottom of your post. Then click on the blue "link" symbol from the top menu. If nothing happens, your computer may be set to not allow scripted windows. If that is the case, a bar may show up at the top that asks you if you'll allow scripted windows. Click on this bar, and then click "Temporarily Allow Scripted Windows." Now, click the "link" symbol again, and this time, a small window should open up that says "Enter the URL." Here, you should enter the URL like this: http://www.yourwebsite.com/archives/PermalinkNumber.

Here is an example of what your link should look like:
http://www.bananapeel.com/archives/125.
After you put your link in, click "Update" and go to your site to see if it works. Make sure you put the right number into the right link, and that the URL is spelled correctly, or it won't work. And, by the way, it only works for published URLs, so make sure you published your post, too, before you try your link.

You may also remember from the chapter about pingbacks and trackbacks that if you put a link in a post, Wordpress will automatically send a pingback to that link. This is great if you are linking to another site, but not so great if you are just linking to your own posts. Receiving pings for linking to your own posts are called "Self-pings." Self-pings are annoying because you have to go in and manually remove them so people can see the pings you have from other blogs, and not just pings within your own blog. Luckily, someone came up with a great solution to this problem, too; a plugin called "No Self Pings." To find it, go to "Plugins," click "Add New," search for "No Self Pings," install it and click "Activate." That is all you have to do to get it to work, and now you won't receive any more self pings when linking posts together.

Anyway, back to the rest of the form. Below the post writing box, you will see a box named "Excerpt." This box is only used if you want to send a trackback to someone, otherwise you can leave it blank. Below "Excerpt," you'll see a box to put your trackback link in, if you have one. The next box is called "Custom fields." You don't have to do anything with this box unless you want to. There is also a link you can click if you want to know more about custom fields.

Scroll down further, and you'll see "Discussion." Hopefully, you have already ticked off the two boxes in this section which allows comments, pingbacks and trackbacks on your posts.

If you decided to install the search engine optimization plugin that I recommended, "All in one SEO pack," you'll see at the bottom of the page a few lines that have to be filled in for each post. Fill in the post title, a short description (less than 160 characters) and a few key words. Then go to the right sidebar where you will see "Tags" and "Categories." It is good to put a few strategic keywords under "Tags" and mark what category you want your post in to make it easier for both the search engine spiders and your readers to find your posts. Once you are done with everything, you can save your draft, preview it, and then click "Publish."

Once you click "Publish," your post will show up in your blog. You can click "Visit Site" at the top of the page if you want to see it. If you don't like what you see, go back to your Wordpress menu under "Posts" and click "Edit." Hover the mouse over your post title, and you'll see the "Edit" button. Click "Edit," make your changes, and click "Update Post" and you're done. You are now officially A BLOGGER!!! Enjoy your freedom of speech – nobody can stop you now!

So, how often do you have to post? As often as possible, within reasonable limits (I personally think that more than once a day is too much), but first, make sure you have something to say that is worth reading. Quality of content is always more important than mere quantity. Hopefully, the ideas will come to you, but if they don't, you might have to go for a walkabout in the blogosphere to look for inspiration from other posts. Technorati is a good place to start, since that is one of the places where you listed your blog anyway. And, if you do come across any interesting blogs, make sure you leave comments to their posts, or at least add a link to their site through your blogroll. This way, readers can find new and interesting sites, and they may even link back to you if they like what you write.

You are finally done creating your blog, and if you are happy with the way it turned out, you

can stop reading now. Enjoy your blogging experience, and go to your Wordpress menu and click on
"StatPress" once in a while to see if anyone is
visiting your blog or signing up for your RSS
feeds. If, however, you would like to know a few
more useful things about what you can do with
your blog, you might want to take a look at the
next few chapters, too. There, I talk about what to
do about spam, how to make money with your
blog, and I also mention another network you
might want to join.

How to Deal With Spam

By now, your blog is up and running. You are blogging away, people are subscribing to your feeds, and everything is looking good. What other concerns do you have to deal with? How about spam?

Believe it or not, but some people have no other interest in life than to annoy others. It isn't just that they are trying to get people to buy their products, or see their dirty porn sites, but some spammers don't even have products to sell! They will just send you ping after ping after ping, all to the same post, and some spammers even make up new names and send their pings from many different URLs! You just feel like writing them back asking them to stop bugging you and get a life, but even that isn't going to stop them. In addition, I just found out that a lot of the spam is actually created by robots just to give you grief. So, what can you do about this?

You have two options: you can download an anti-spam plugin of some kind, or you can black-list the URLs that are offending you. The easiest thing to do is to simply blacklist the spam-URLs. Here is what you do:

Log in to your Wordpress dashboard and go to "Comments." This is where all your pings, trackbacks and comments are listed. Under each comment listing you will see an 11-digit number (some may be shorter, but that's ok). This is the URL that the ping or comment was sent from. Copy this number. Then go to "Settings" and click on "Discussion." Scroll down until you see "Comment Blacklist." Paste your URL into the window, one on each line, then scroll down, and click "Save Changes." This will effectively block any message, comment or ping that comes from that URL. Just be aware that if you blacklist the URLs, they'll end up in your spam section in Wordpress, and you'll have to go in and delete them manually before they become too many. You can find your spam posts if you click on "Comments" in your Wordpress menu, then click the "Spam" tab at the top of the page, and it will give you the option to delete them.

If you get tired of checking for spam every day, you might want to download an anti-spam plugin that will solve the problem more permanently. There are many plugins that can do this, and after reading through all the descriptions, I chose one called WP-spamfree. It is compatible with the latest version of Wordpress, it is easy to install, it will allow you to install a spam-free contact form if you wish, and it even comes with a widget for the sidebar that will show how many spam comments have been eliminated. If you want to install this plugin, go to "Plugins" and click "Add New." Search for "WP-spamfree," install it and activate it. In the plugins menu, you can click on "Settings" if you want to change anything, or you can just leave all the default settings as they are. If you want to add the spam counter in one of your sidebars, just go to "Appearance," click on "Widgets" and then click on "Add" next to the "WP-spamfree Counter" widget. Once it shows up in the sidebar where you want it, just click "Save Changes" and you're done.

The bad thing about the internet is that all kinds of perverted, creepy, nasty people lurk around out there. On the good side, the net is a place where you can find information about absolutely anything you want to know, and you can express yourself as freely as you want. Having your own blog gives you **total freedom of speech,** because nobody else can moderate your blog! So, basically, we just have to take the good with the bad, and deal with spam whenever it happens. Blogging is a fun thing to do, so don't let the spam get in your way. Just blacklist the URLs, or simply download your favorite anti-spam plugin, and keep on blogging!

Making Money

A girl's got to live (I know, boys do to!); it is as simple as that. Blogs appeal to creative people, and creative people have lots of ideas and skills that they might want to promote. After all, the internet isn't just a place for exchanging information, it is also a place where you can sell your products or services without having to rent a shop space and pay thousands of dollars in overhead every month.

More and more people are shopping online every month, since the advantages far outweigh the disadvantages. If you can find what you want while shopping in your pajamas, why would you want to go to the mall and risk getting your car stolen while you are shopping inside? Chances are, you won't even find what you are looking for in a store, since no store can carry enough inventoriy to please everyone. So, the natural solution is to shop on the net, and even in difficult times, when the economy is going through great transitions, internet sales are still up. Therefore, your blog is not just a place to express yourself with words; it can also be a way to express yourself through one of your many talents.

Some people are totally against making money with your blog, but, oh, well, what can I say? There are purists and fanatics everywhere, and they are entitled to their own opinions, I guess, as long as they don't enforce them onto anyone else. So, if you belong to the purist category, you don't have to read the rest of this chapter, but for the rest of us, who do need to pay some bills once in a while, keep on reading!

So, what are the options for making money with a blog? Well, if you don't mind advertising on your blog, you can always sign up with Google AdSense. Just log into your Google account, and you'll see a link to "Adsense" at the bottom of the page.

Google AdSense is a free program that creates dynamic contextual ads in your content pages, or in your feeds and search pages. Contextual advertising means that they try to match the advertising with the content in your posts, so that the products are relevant to what you are talking about. The advertising is also dynamic, which means that a different image shows up every time the page loads. That way, people don't have to look at the same boring advertising ads every time they go to your blog. You can even download a Wordpress plugin called "AdSense Integrator" to help you manage your AdSense ads if you wish.

So, the essential question is, how do you get paid? With Google AdSense you can get paid either with cost-per-click (CPC) or cost-per-1000-impressions (CPM). If you choose CPC, Google's advertisers will pay a certain fee for every person that clicks on one of the advertisements in your blog. If you choose CPM, they pay a fee based on how many times the ads are run on your site, which might be good if you have a lot of visitors. Who knows which is best? You may have to just try it and see for yourself which option you like better.

There are many other advertising companies out there, too, and they all work in slightly different ways. You might want to check out blogads.com, payperpost.com and also federated-media.com at some point.

Blogads is "a network of influential bloggers who collaborate to promote and sell blog advertising." So, if you go with blogads, you could end up both buying and selling ads.

Federated Media is an exclusive, invitation-only advertising network that accepts only blogs with "passion, authority, integrity and strong community support." If you fit this category, it might be worth your while to contact them. But, if you are still just a new blogger, forget Federated Media for now.

Payperpost is another interesting advertising opportunity. After you sign up with this company, and they approve your blog, they give you what they call "opportunities." The opportunities are your chance to write a post about a product and keep the post on your site for 30 days. It doesn't have to be on your front page, but it does have to be live for 30 days. If 30 days after you wrote about their product, the post is still live, you get paid for what you wrote, and then you can delete the post.

But, advertising is not the only way to make money with your blog. You may have skills or products you can sell as well. If you do, you can advertise your skills, services or products in one of your sidebars, if you wish, or you can create a static page with information about what you are selling instead. If you like to write articles, you can even advertise your writing services by offering to write articles for people who are too busy to write for their own blogs. They tell you what they want you to write, and you set your price. The more famous and sought after your articles get, the more money you can ask for each assignment. However, if you are selling anything on your blog, the big question is still, how do you get paid?

If you want to get paid the easy way, with no monthly fees, Paypal is the greatest! I know that some of you might have some issues about Paypal, but when you see how easy it is go get paid, you simply have to get over your reservations.

You don't have to be a rocket scientist to open a Paypal account. All you have to do is go to http://www.paypal.com and click the "Signup" link at the top of the page. Fill in the forms and give them your bank account information as well as a creditcard number. (Don't worry, your information is totally safe, as long as you don't give anyone your password!) After you sign up, Paypal will deposit two small amounts into your bank account, usually less than a dollar. When the amounts show up in your bank account, write down the amounts, then log back into your Paypal account, and find a link to confirm your account. Click on this link, fill in the two amounts, click "Confirm" and you are done. Paypal has now confirmed that this really IS your bank account.

Similarly, they also have to confirm your credit card. (Make sure that your credit card's billing address corresponds with your own address). After signing up, you will see in your credit card account on the internet a couple of charges pending for $1.00 each from Paypal, but don't worry; they won't actually charge the money. After a few days, the charges magically disappear. The main purpose for this is to find out if your credit card is valid. Once Paypal knows, you are good to go.

The biggest problem with Paypal doesn't actually have anything to do with Paypal itself – it has to do with spammers that flood your email with fake messages, supposedly from Paypal, that states that your account has been compromised, and that they need all your information, such as passwords, etc. NEVER, EVER fall for this scheme! If you have any doubts, open a new window in your browser, put http://www.paypal.com into the address bar and enter your account from the normal Paypal homepage. If there is something wrong with your account, it will say so as soon as you log in. If you don't see any warnings, your account is fine! Just promise to NEVER log in through an email, and your Paypal account won't give you any grief.

So, why do you need a Paypal account? Besides the fact that it allows you to shop until you drop on Ebay, **Paypal also offers free shopping buttons for your products or services**. Here what you do to get a Paypal shopping button:

Log in to your Paypal account. Click on the "Products and Services" tab at the top of the page. Under "Ways to Get Paid," click on "Website Payments Standard." Here you will get several options:

1) A "Buy Now" button for single items
2) An "Add to Cart" button for multiple items
3) A "Subscribe" button for automated payments.

4) You'll also get the option to add a dona-
tion button or a gift certificate if you
wish.

And the best thing is, all of this is com-
pletely free and customizable. After picking what
you want and filling in the necessary information,
Paypal will create a code that you can paste
somewhere on your website or blog. Very professional, and with no effort or cost! Paypal will
allow people to pay any way they like, with all
kinds of credit cards, easy and convenient.

Whenever anyone buys one of your products, you instantly get a message from Paypal in
your email that states that you have received
money, and also who sent it, and what they paid
for. It is so easy – I love it! You can even edit the
shopping button later, if your needs change! Here
is what you do to edit your Paypal shopping
button:

Log in to your Paypal account and click
"Profile" at the top of the home page. Under
"Selling Preferences," click on "My Saved Buttons." Pick the button you want to edit, click the
dropdown menu at the end of that line and click
"Edit Button." Make your changes and click the
"Save Changes" button at the bottom of the page.
Then you just copy your new code and paste it
back on your blog page. No sweat! Finally something that is easy, free and consumer friendly! So
if you are dreaming about running your own
business, Paypal is definitely the way to go! It is
free, it is easy, it is convenient, and it looks professional. Who could possibly want anything
more?

BlogHer

If you are a girl, you should definitely check out blogher.com. Blogher is a networking community that gives women the opportunity to write for each other and connect. I have heard Blogher described as a place where there are blogs "by women, for women and to women."

The whole thing started in 2005 when 3 girls got together and arranged a blogger conference for women to answer the question of "Where are the women bloggers?" The conference was so successful that the women who came made it clear that they wanted to "meet" every day, and that was the beginning of BlogHer.com.

BlogHer has over 9000 blogs by and for women in their blogrolls. These blogs are categorized into about 20 different categories. In addition, there are over 50 different editors that cover every category and constantly tell you what is hot in the blogosphere. That way, your blog and your posts can easily be found, even though you just started blogging.

In BlogHer, you don't even have to try to fit into an interest group if you don't want to; you are actually encouraged to follow all of your interests! It is a place where diversity of topics is appreciated, and a place where you can go to for advice and support on anything that is an issue in your life!

Joining BlogHer is easy. All that is required is that you have a valid email address and user name, you have to be a girl, (or a guy writing specifically for women), and your blog should be at least 30 days old. Before it shows up in the blog-rolls, it also has to be approved by one of the editors. This is to ensure that your blog has qual-ity content and isn't just a spam site.

So, if you want to join the girls at BlogHer, this is what you have to do: First, go to http://www.blogher.com. To join, click on the "Join Us" tab in the right sidebar. Fill in first name, last name, user name and email address. Read the fascinating terms and conditions, accept them and click "Create New Account."

After creating your account, you can log in and go to "MyBlogHer" and click on "Settings." Under "Account Settings" you can upload a pic-ture for your profile. Then you can go into "Public Profile" to write your bio. People love bios, so don't skip this part. You can also fill in tags, list all your other blogs, if any, and you can change the settings and themes. If you click on "Create a Post" you can write a post, or you can even list a book you have written that will show up in Blog-Her's library section. At the bottom of this page, it will also tell you how to submit your blog to Blog-Her's blogroll. Blogher is a fun place to hang out, so if you feel inspired to join and submit your blog, go for it.

So, what do you have to do to be a good blogger? Simple: **Read, write and participate**, and slowly, slowly, your blog will start to develop its own following. Compared to having a website, I was amazed at how quickly people actually started finding my blog. With a website, it can take months before anyone stumbles upon it, and some websites are so lost in space that nobody ever finds them. Blogs, however, are very different animals. People can find your blog, even the day you write your first post, probably thanks to automatic pinging of important sites! So what are you waiting for? The world is ready for what you have to say, so go and turn on your computer and see what ideas come to you – you might even surprise yourself...

Other Blogging Books Worth Reading

Problogger, Secrets for Blogging Your Way to a Six-Figure Income, by Darren Rowse and Chris Garrett

The writing style in this book is easy to read, and the author tells his story and shares all his hints, tips, secrets and good advice with the reader. Well worth reading.

IT Girl's Guide to Blogging with Moxie, by Joelle Reeder & Katherine Scoleri

Not only are these two ladies way cool, but they sure know what they are talking about as well. The book contains a lot of information that is different enough from Problogger that it is not a bad idea to actually buy both of these books.

Index

Index

Index

optimize, 15, 41, 65

options menu, 26, 31, 32, 34, 37

P

parent pages, 48

Paypal, 94, 95, 96

Paypal shopping button, 95, 96

paypal.com, 94, 95

payperpost.com, 93

permalinks, 47, 79, 81

php sheet, 47, 48

pingbacks, 61, 62, 63, 64, 66, 75, 78, 82, 83

pinging, 2, 60, 99

plugin, 39, 40, 41, 42, 45, 49, 57, 73, 83, 87, 88, 89, 92

plugins, 39, 40, 41, 43, 45, 51, 57, 79, 88

posts, 8, 42, 49, 53, 54, 57, 61, 66, 71, 75, 77, 78, 79, 81, 82, 83, 84, 88, 92, 97

R

Really Simple Syndication, 53

register.com, 10

reserved, 2

RSS, 1, 53, 54, 56, 57, 58, 67, 77, 85

S

scripted windows, 82

search engines, 9, 13, 14, 15, 32, 41, 65

self-hosted, 7, 8

self-pings, 83

server, 49, 56

sidebar.php, 58

sidebars, 26, 27, 31, 47, 57, 77, 89, 93

Simple Scripts, 1, 12, 21, 23

slug, 75, 76

spam, 10, 59, 62, 85, 87, 88, 89, 98

Index

W

wavatars, 1, 71, 73, 74

website, 7, 13, 17, 21, 29, 48, 59, 62, 65, 96, 98

websites, 1, 9, 65, 99

whois-search, 17

widgets, 57

Wordpress, 1, 2, 1, 2, 3, 4, 11, 12, 21, 22, 23, 25, 26, 27, 29, 30, 31, 34, 35, 39, 40, 41, 45, 48, 49, 50, 51, 57, 58, 60, 61, 63,

68, 73, 74, 75, 78, 79, 81, 82, 84, 85, 88, 92

wordpressbackup.com, 50

Wordtracker.com, 14, 15

wp-content, 29, 33, 34

Y

Yet Another Related Post, 42

Z

zip file, 2, 49

Index

Breinigsville, PA USA
07 December 2009
228798BV00002B/88/P